IMAGES
of Aviation

THE
DE HAVILLAND
AIRCRAFT COMPANY

Geoffrey de Havilland at the controls of his Biplane No. 2 which flew successfully in 1910.

Front cover illustration:
A D.H.9 being prepared for an operational flight in France in 1918.

IMAGES
of Aviation

THE
DE HAVILLAND
AIRCRAFT COMPANY

Compiled by
Maurice F. Allward and John W.R. Taylor OBE

TEMPUS

First published 1996, reprinted 1999
Copyright © Maurice Allward and John Taylor, 1996

Tempus Publishing Limited
The Mill, Brimscombe Port,
Stroud, Gloucestershire, GL5 2QG

Arcadia Publishing
2 Cumberland Street
Charlston, SC 29401

ISBN 0 7524 0630 2

Typesetting and origination by
Tempus Publishing Limited
Printed in Great Britain by
Midway Clark Printing, Wiltshire

*Dedicated to the memory
of
Geoffrey de Havilland
and the Enterprise he
created at Hatfield*

Acknowledgements

A book of this nature cannot be the work of authors alone, for without the photographs it could not have been produced. The authors, therefore, wish to thank their many friends and those companies who have supplied the majority of the photographs.

Friends who loaned photographs include: Philip Birtles, Alan Copas, Derek James, Ken Munson, Nigel Price, Reg Redford, John Stroud and Louis Vosloo, to whom we extend our sincere thanks.

Companies who kindly supplied photographs are, first and formost, the de Havilland Aircraft Company. Others include: British Aerospace, British Petroleum, the de Havilland Heritage Museum, *Flight*, KLM, Klee Oakwood Grange Collection and the Royal Aircraft Establishment.

Maurice Allward and John Taylor
Hatfield and Surbiton, July 1996

Contents

Geoffrey de Havilland's first aeroplane, clearly built of less than robust materials, under construction in his workshop in Fulham in 1909. It was assembled and flown, briefly, in a small field at Seven Barrows, Hampshire.

Introduction

Geoffrey de Havilland's first aeroplane was built in a small workshop in Fulham, financed by an advance on the £1,000 that a farsighted grandfather had intended to leave him in his will. He was assisted by a young engineer named Frank Hearle, who was content to take a cut in the ninepence-halfpenny an hour he had been earning as a bus mechanic. They were looked after by de Havilland's sister Ione, who later became Mrs Hearle. The aeroplane's fabric covering was stitched on a hand sewing machine by the designer's wife, Louie.

The tools used to build aircraft No.1 from locally purchased whitewood cost less than £20. A 45 hp engine of de Havilland's own design was built for £250 by the Iris Car Company. When the aeroplane was completed, it was taken to Seven Barrows in Hampshire, a few miles from the family home at Crux Eaton. The designer eased it off the ground in December 1909, but not for long. The frail wings crumpled and it crashed, without injury to the pilot, although only the engine and one of the propellers were worth salvaging from the wreckage.

Geoffrey de Havilland quickly built a more robust biplane of straight-grained spruce and ash, this time with a single pusher propeller. When No.2 was taken to Seven Barrows it showed promise. Lying flat on the ground, Frank Hearle could see clear space between grass and wheels as the biplane passed him at 25-30 mph. Encouraged, de Havilland gradually taught himself to fly until, on 10 September 1910, he was able to remain airborne for a quarter of a mile. Soon, he was sufficiently confident to carry Hearle as a passenger, followed by Louie and his eight-week-old son Geoffrey, who must have been the youngest person in the world to have flown in an aeroplane at that time.

The advance from grandfather Jason Saunders was now exhausted. By a happy coincidence, in October 1910, the British War Office announced that the scope of the Balloon Section of the Royal Engineers was to be extended 'to afford opportunities for aeroplaning'. Nobody explained where the aeroplanes were to come from. Superintendent Mervyn O'Gorman of the Balloon Factory

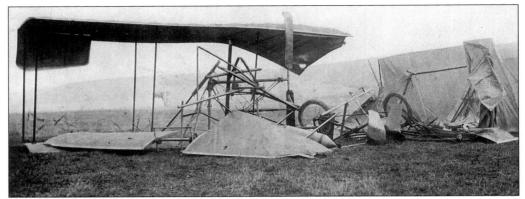

The remains of Geoffrey de Havilland's Biplane No. 1 after it stalled and crashed on its first, and only, flight in December 1909. The pilot was uninjured and the engine salvaged.

at Farnborough was persuaded by his engineer in charge of design, Frederick Green, to buy de Havilland's No.2 biplane for £400 and take on its builder as a designer and test pilot.

When the War Office sent to the Factory for repair a French Blériot monoplane that had become known as 'the Man Killer', permission was obtained to rebuild rather than repair it. The original engine was retained, but what had come to Farnborough as a tractor (front-propeller) monoplane emerged eventually as a tail-first pusher biplane known as the S.E.1. A similar 'repair' transformed a Voisin pusher into a neat tractor biplane without even its original engine. Redesignated B.E.1, this machine's 60 hp Renault ran so quietly that it was known as 'the Silent Aeroplane'.

By the time the Royal Flying Corps came into being in 1912, the B.E.1 had been developed by Green and de Havilland into the much improved B.E.2, which was put into production by private manufacturers for both the RFC and Royal Naval Air Service. Further changes, by E.T. Busk, met the Army's wish for an aircraft so stable in flight that its pilot could take his hands off the controls and write a reconnaissance report. Senior officers and bureaucrats saw little use for aeroplanes beyond reconnaissance, and the RFC was to receive more than 3,000 of the inherently stable B.E.2s for use in the First World War.

It was tragic blunder. When the Germans invented an interrupter gear that enabled a machine gun to fire forward between the spinning propeller blades of their Fokker monoplanes, the B.E.2s lacked the quick reaction agility to escape them. The gun supplied to the observer in the front cockpit was of little use, as its field of fire was obstructed by the wings. The Royal Flying Corps was almost shot from the skies over France during this 'Fokker Scourge' of 1915 and 1916.

Geoffrey de Havilland played a prominent part in regaining the initiative for the RFC. At Farnborough, under the Factory's quaint designation system, his No. 2 biplane had become the F.E.1 (Farman Experimental No.1) because its pusher configuration resembled that of widely used French Farman aircraft. His first all-new design at the Factory was the improved F.E.2, still with a pusher propeller behind the wings. After it had been fitted with a fabric-covered cockpit and nose-mounted machine gun, it pioneered a way of firing forward that did not need interrupter gear.

Well over two years were lost before the fully developed two-seat F.E.2b completely equipped No. 20 Squadron RFC in France, in January 1916. In 1914 de Havilland had been pressured into taking the job of Inspector of Aircraft at Farnborough. Dismayed at losing his design duties, he had resigned and joined George Holt Thomas's newly formed Aircraft Manufacturing Company (Airco). From the start, the aircraft he designed there became known as D.H. rather than Airco types. The two-seat D.H.1 reconnaissance pusher was followed by a much smaller and highly manoeuvrable single-seater on the same F.E.2-style lines. The prototype of this D.H.2 completed its flight testing in July 1915, just as the Fokkers were beginning to make their presence felt, and was hastened into production. When No. 24 Squadron flew its D.H.2s to France in February 1916, it was the first RFC single-seat fighter squadron deployed to any war theatre.

The D.H.2s and F.E.2bs were too late to save the hapless B.E.2 squadrons but, in partnership with French Nieuport Babies, they out-fought the Fokker monoplanes until new tractor biplane fighters with interrupter gear could take over.

Meanwhile, Airco turned its attention to producing a bomber that could punish Germany for the destruction that Zeppelin airships were beginning to inflict on England. The D.H.3 twin-engined bomber was rejected by the War Office, which considered strategic bombing not worth the effort. By the time German bombers changed the official mind, Geoffrey de Havilland had switched to the single-engined D.H.4 that is regarded as the finest day bomber of the First World War.

Other fighters, bombers and training aircraft followed, but the Armistice

With rare good fortune, somebody with a camera captured the moment when Geoffrey de Havilland took off from the field at Seven Barrows in his Biplane No. 2 on 10 September 1910. Before long, he was flying figures of eight and staying in the air for several minutes.

Biplane No. 2 at Farnborough in 1911, after it had been purchased by the War Office for £400 and redesignated F.E.1.

necessitated a change of tack in 1918. Most military contracts were cancelled overnight. Famous manufacturers, including Airco, went out of business. The pioneer airlines that tried to establish passenger services were content to use crude conversions of surplus military aircraft, and were not in the market for anything new and expensive. Despite this, Geoffrey de Havilland decided to form his own company. Frank Hearle, his fellow-worker from the Fulham era, was invited to be Works Manager. Other members of his top team had all been with him at Airco. They were to stay together until well after the Second World War.

Airco put up £10,000 of a total capital of under £20,000. Thus, on 25 September 1920, The de Havilland Aircraft Company Ltd was registered with a working capital of £1,875, a small amount of work transferred from Airco and what its founder described as 'perhaps an unwarranted degree of optimism'.

The 1920 works was established in two small buildings on a field at the end of Stag Lane in Edgware that had served as a wartime training aerodrome. The first British airlines were already operating out of Hounslow and Cricklewood to the Continent, using mostly converted D.H.4s and 9s. Far more civilised was Airco's D.H.18. Eight passengers travelled in a proper cabin in the plywood covered fuselage with the pilot in an open cockpit above and behind, rather like the driver of one of London's old horse drawn Hansom cabs.

The de Havilland Aircraft Company took over completion of two D.H.18s. It also had an Air Ministry contract to build a wooden cantilever monoplane to carry up to ten passengers. The resulting D.H. 29 did not handle well; redesign and testing would clearly take time. So, with two of the UK's pioneer operators,

Daimler Hire and Instone Air Line, desperate to buy better equipment, it was decided to revert to the well proven all-wood biplane formula. The D.H.34 was, to a large degree, a D.H.18 with the pilot forward of the wings. With Instone, it became the first airliner in the world to carry a uniformed steward able to serve refreshments in flight.

A de Havilland Aeroplane Hire Service was opened in 1921 with a fleet of D.H.9Bs and Cs. Two years later the de Havilland School of Flying was formed as one of four schools entrusted with training and maintaining the proficiency of RAF Reservists. Those it taught to fly included Geoffrey de Havilland's sons, Geoffrey and Peter, soon joined in the Reserve by their brother John. A de Havilland Aeronautical Technical School came into being in 1928.

The RAF had inaugurated a Desert Air Mail service between Cairo and Baghdad in 1920, using D.H.10 twin-engined bombers. When Imperial Airways absorbed four of Britain's pioneer airlines in 1924, the Government decided to transfer this operation to civilian control and to encourage the planning of long-haul services that might one day link Britain with the farthest Dominions.

Spectacular survey flights to India, Australia and South Africa were made by Alan Cobham, one of Britain's greatest pioneer pilots, in a D.H.50. Little more than another civil development of the D.H.4/D.H.9 family, with a cabin for four passengers, it began its career by winning a civil aeroplane competition in Sweden with 999 marks out of a possible 1,000, and was flown to victory by Cobham in the 1924 King's Cup Air Race. Later, D.H.50s became particular

Geoffrey de Havilland became an assistant designer and test pilot at Farnborough, where he was responsible for the tail-first S.E.1 pusher biplane in 1911. Before he could remedy its shortcomings an official at the Royal Aircraft Factory, who had held a pilot's licence for only a week, insisted on flying it, crashed and was killed.

Stag Lane, home of the newly formed de Havilland Aircraft Company, in 1921. Circled is one of the two original sheds used as general offices. When Stag Lane closed the shed was moved to Hatfield, where it served as a museum for de Havilland artifacts until closure of this site in the early 1990s. The shed is being preserved for eventual display in the de Havilland Heritage Centre.

favourites of airlines in Australia, where they were built under licence.

The transport built at Stag Lane for the Desert Air Mail operation was the three-engined D.H.66 Hercules. It was to give splendid service, but development proved difficult. The company had to learn to use steel tube construction, instead of its familiar wood, for the large fabric-covered fuselage, although the seven to fourteen passengers and baggage were still housed in plywood 'boxes' suspended inside. To make matters worse, the Government thought it would be a good idea to produce a bomber based on the Hercules. They asked for so many successive design changes that de Havilland gave up, and responsibility for the D.H.67 was transferred to the Gloster Aircraft Company, as were the far larger D.H.72 bomber and the D.H.77 single-seat monoplane interceptor designed to 1927 official requirements. The de Havilland Aircraft Company was convinced that life would be far happier if it stayed with wooden aeroplanes for the civilian market. So began the company's golden era.

The upsurge in fortune was sparked by light aeroplane trials organised in 1923/24 by the *Daily Mail* newspaper and the Air Ministry. Two single-seat D.H.53 Humming Birds specially built to compete did not win prizes, but so impressed officials by their ability to fly 59 miles on a gallon of petrol, and to perform loops and rolls never before attempted with such diminutive aeroplanes, that eight were bought for the RAF. Pilots at the Central Flying School found them fun to fly; Alan Cobham was less impressed when his D.H.53 was passed by a railway train while flying into a headwind over Belgium.

Geoffrey de Havilland realised that a more practical, higher-powered, two-seater was required by the flying clubs that the Air Ministry was keen to sponsor. He persuaded Frank Halford of the Aircraft Disposal Company to cut in half one of its huge stock of twenty-five shilling, eight-cylinder Vee Renault-type engines, and then design a new crankcase and cylinder head. The result was the four-cylinder in-line Cirrus I that gave 60 hp for the weight of only 290 lb. Around this, the team at Stag Lane designed the prototype Moth – named to reflect Geoffrey de Havilland's renown as a lepidopterist, which inspired the moth's-wing fin and rudder shape of so many of his designs.

The Moth could be bought for £595, flown by almost anybody, towed behind a car and kept in a garage. Three years later it even had its own engine, the 80 hp Gipsy, designed by Halford, who was appointed chief designer of the newly-formed de Havilland Engine Division. Moths made possible a worldwide flying club movement and turned Amy Johnson into a national heroine when she

Standard 2-gallon cans of motor spirit were used at Croydon Airport in the mid-1920s to refuel this D.H.50J. Registered G-EBFO, it became famous as the aircraft in which Alan Cobham gained a well deserved knighthood making long-distance survey flights on behalf of Imperial Airways.

A large crowd welcomed the Imperial Airways D.H.66 Hercules that carried Sir Samuel Hoare, Britain's Air Minister, and Lady Maud Hoare to Delhi on 8 January 1927. This inaugural flight marked the transfer of the RAF's pioneer Desert Air Mail service from military to civil control. Lady Irwin, wife of the Viceroy of India, named G-EBMX *City of Delhi*.

flew one solo to Australia. This was only one of countless great flights in Moths, which became standard trainers of the Royal Australian Air Force and were built in Australia, Finland, France and the USA.

By 1929, Stag Lane was building sixteen a week; its payroll had grown from 300 to 1,500, with subsidiaries in Australia and Canada. From the Moth evolved a succession of famous lightplanes, beginning with the 120 hp Gipsy-engined Puss Moth monoplane. In one of these, with two huge extra fuel tanks, Jim Mollison crossed the Atlantic at a fuel and oil cost of £11 1s 3d, years before airlines were able to attempt such a flight. Best remembered of all the Moth's successors is, perhaps, the Tiger Moth, on which a high proportion of the pilots of the Second World War gained their wings and which can still be seen flying all over the world in the mid-1990s.

In 1934, the company moved its headquarters from Stag Lane to a new factory at Hatfield. From there came the D.H.88 Comet racer that won the greatest-ever air race, from England to Australia, in 1934. Airlines bought in hundreds wooden biplane transports like the D.H.84 Dragon, D.H.86 and D.H.89 Dragon Rapide. The beautiful D.H.91 Albatross was an attempt to use the D.H.88 Comet experience to produce a 200 mph four-engined transport for twenty-two passengers. It was a wooden airliner too far, and the twelve-to-seventeen-passenger D.H.95 Flamingo of 1938 became the first all-metal aeroplane built by de Havilland.

It was not the end of the road for wood. The all-wooden Mosquito is remembered as one of the truly remarkable combat aircraft of the Second World

War, and even the first de Havilland jet fighter had a wooden fuselage. But there were to be no postwar successors to the Moth. Instead, it was the company's new skills in metal construction that made possible the Dove and Heron small airliners, and the Comet jet airliner that survived immense setbacks in opening up the whole new vista of world air travel for ordinary folk.

As its original 'family circle' of directors retired one by one, the de Havilland Aircraft Company gradually slipped towards the financially obsessive world of the 1980s and '90s, in which the priority of very different people is to make money rather than aeroplanes. Under government policy that merged Britain's aircraft manufacturers into major groupings, de Havilland became, first, a division of Hawker Siddeley Aviation in 1959. Its famous name survived in Britain for a while, only to disappear when British Aerospace came into being in 1977.

Sir Geoffrey de Havilland, knighted in 1944, died on 21 May 1965; his test pilot sons, John and Geoffrey, had been killed in flying accidents. Hatfield closed. Of the last aircraft designed there, the D.H.121 Trident was retired, the D.H.125 programme was sold to Raytheon of the USA and the BAe 146 production line was transferred north to Manchester, in a first step leading towards a Franco-Italian-British partnership with its headquarters at Toulouse in France. Until memories fade, engineers around the globe will continue to assert, with pride, that they worked for de Havilland in the days when British aviation set the pace for the world.

The fully developed de Havilland factory at Hatfield in the 1960s. To the right is the recently completed three-storey New Design Block. In the left background is the new flight test shed, with a Comet airliner on the apron.

One
War in Europe

At the outbreak of the First World War in 1914, Geoffrey de Havilland was called up for service with No. 2 Squadron of the Royal Flying Corps at Farnborough. Fortunately the War Office soon realised his potential as an aircraft designer. He was promoted to Captain and returned to work with Airco at Hendon where, as Chief Designer, he became responsible for a succession of combat aircraft. These included the D.H.4, a bomber with the speed of a fighter that had no equal, enemy or allied, in its day. At the wartime peak more than ninety firms contributed to the production of de Havilland aircraft, with output from Airco alone reaching 300 a month in 1918.

Aircraft designed by de Havilland served in all combat areas. On the Western Front, D.H.2s did good work during the awesome Battle of the Somme, helping to end the scourge of Germany's Fokker monoplanes. The D.H.4 first saw action during the Battle of Arras and later bombed German factories. In 1918 this type backed up the big British attack at Amiens and took reconnaissance photographs of German defences around Zeebrugge and Ostend. On the Home Front, a D.H.4 shot down Zeppelin L.70 on its way to bomb England and damaged L.65 enough to make it turn for its home base. Other D.H.4s served in the Aegean Islands, Greece and North Russia.

When the Armistice was signed in 1918, the Royal Air Force had a strength of 22,647 aircraft. Of these 3,877 were de Havilland types, including 2,271 D.H.9s and D.H.9As.

Previous pages: Almost 6,300 D.H.4 day bombers were built in Britain and the USA, and are numbered among the most successful aircraft of the First World War.

The first aeroplane designed by Geoffrey de Havilland after joining the Aircraft Manufacturing Company was the D.H.1 two-seat reconnaissance biplane, armed with a forward-firing machine gun. It saw little active use, even though seventy-three were delivered to the Royal Flying Corps and were not withdrawn from service until the end of 1918.

The prototype of the D.H.2 single-seater fighter, first flown by Geoffrey de Havilland on 1 June 1915. The pusher layout was retained because no British interrupter gear was yet available to allow machine guns to fire forward between the blades of a spinning propeller.

The D.H.2 was very manoeuvrable and had a good rate of climb; it was used by pilots to develop the attacking technique of aiming their whole aircraft at targets. The flag on the wing of this D.H.2 shows that it is a flight commander's machine.

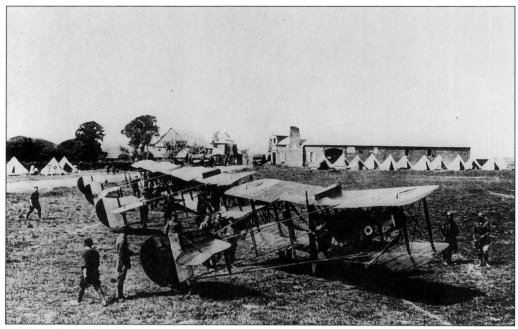

D.H.2s, shown here ready for action on a French airfield, contributed significantly to the establishment of Allied air superiority during the Battle of the Somme in 1916. Major L.W.B. Rees of No. 32 Squadron, RFC, was awarded the Victoria Cross for attacking single-handedly a formation of ten German two-seaters, two of which were forced down.

The little D.H.2 is best remembered as one of the types that ended the scourge of Germany's Fokker monoplanes that had almost shot the RFC from the skies in France. Thirty-two served in the near East, 266 on Europe's Western Front.

Only this prototype of the D.H.3 twin-engined, long-range bomber and a single improved D.H.3A were flown. The three-man crew included two gunners, each with twin machine guns; bomb load was 680 lb and the aircraft could fly for eight hours. Unfortunately, the War Office of the time considered strategic bombing a waste of effort and cancelled a contract for fifty D.H.3As.

The D.H.3 was a large aeroplane with a wing span of nearly 61 feet, but its wings could be folded to fit into the hangars of 1916.

An early production D.H.4 day bomber with a Rolls-Royce engine. Its handling qualities were superb and, with a maximum speed of up to 143 mph in later versions, nothing could catch it when it flew at heights greater than 15,000 ft. The major problem was that the two cockpits were too far apart for the crew to coordinate their defence and were separated by a large and very vulnerable fuel tank.

Without crew, fuel and weapons, a D.H.4 weighed barely more than one ton, and could be manhandled by a squad of eight ground crew. This aircraft has the taller undercarriage fitted to later D.H.4s to prevent damage to the propeller by ground contact during take-off.

British production lines like this delivered a total of 1,449 D.H.4s. A further 3,227 had been manufactured in the USA by the time of the Armistice, of which 1,885 had been shipped to France. No aircraft of USA design fought on the Western Front in the First World War and the Americans continued building D.H.4s post-war.

An observer's view looking forward from the rear cockpit of a D.H.4 flying over the battlelines in France.

A D.H.4 over the Western Front, 1917. This photograph was taken by Lieutenant Alan Curtis from another D.H.4.

The D.H.5 was the first de Havilland fighter to take advantage of the Constantinesco interrupter gear that at last enabled machine guns on Allied aircraft to be fired forward through the propeller disc. In an effort to retain the excellent pilot's field of view forward offered by earlier pusher layouts, it had a back-staggered upper wing. Nearly 500 entered service, but the D.H.5 was outflown above 10,000 ft by enemy fighters which usually attacked from the rear where the view was very poor. It was usually relegated to ground attack duties in 1917, the good view forward assisting this role.

To meet the ever increasing need of the Royal Flying Corps for more pilots, this first of two prototype D.H.6 primary trainers began its test flying in 1916. Apart from what was becoming the traditional D.H. curved fin and rudder, the emphasis was on straight lines and square tips to simplify production. Apprehensive pupil pilots nicknamed their aircraft 'The Clutching Hand' because of the heavily cambered wings; but the D.H.6 served its purpose well. More than 300 of the 2,282 built ended the war on anti-submarine patrol around Britain's coastline.

The D.H.9 was intended to be an improvement over the D.H.4 (in the background). The cockpits were no longer widely separated, enabling the observer to coordinate combat tactics with the pilot. However, the under-powered D.H.9 was never good enough to replace the earlier bomber, and the search for a replacement for its unreliable Puma engine became urgent when the production lines began completing one aircraft every forty minutes somewhere in Britain.

A Puma-engined D.H.9 being prepared for an operational flight in France in 1918.

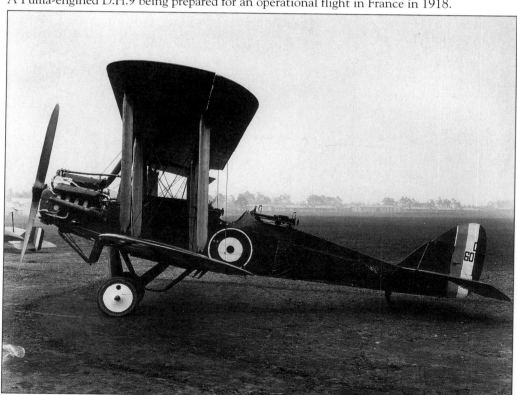

Among new engines flown in D.H.9s was the prototype water-cooled Napier Lion with a heated carburettor fitted to testbed aircraft C6078 at Farnborough in 1918.

A cask of Somerset cider being loaded into the rear cockpit of a Westland-built D.H.4 at Yeovil. The bombers were delivered direct to a Royal Naval Air Service squadron in Belgium and when flown solo required ballast in the rear cockpit. Conveniently, it was found that a cask of cider was just about the weight needed.

Year 1918 Month / Date	AIRCRAFT Type	No.	Pilot, or 1st Pilot	2nd Pilot, Pupil or Passenger	DUTY (Including Results and Remarks)
—	—	—	—	—	254·55 Totals Brought Forward 223·35 As Pilot.
June 7 1918	D.H.9	C 6114	Lt. A.H.C.	Sgt. A.W. Davies (Farewell to C6114) (In this fight with the 'Circus' our formation of 7 lost 1 & bagged 5 Huns.)	to one man having engine trouble. 5 Huns about. Bombed FLAVY. After dropping bombs, a piece of 'Archie' went through radiator. 40·45 Huns then attacked, scoring many hits, as we were in rear of formation of 7. Davies got one out of control. We lost 1 – & Huns 5. Engine seized solid at 5000'. Huns broke off & turned back when near our lines & we glided S.W & made good landing in wheat field, but all ailerons dropped as compensating cable was shot thro'. Holes in gravity tank, under my seat through fuselage, wings & in prop. 2 tailplane bracing wires shot through. Discovered that Davies also lived at Golders Green's.

Log book extract covering the engagement of Lt Alan Curtis in his D.H.9 C6114 on 7 June 1918 with between forty and forty-five aircraft of von Richthofen's famous Flying Circus.

Drawing prepared by Lt Alan Curtis depicting his engagement with aircraft of von Richthofen's Flying Circus. During the dogfight his D.H.9 was hit in the radiator by anti-aircraft shrapnel and crash-landed just inside the Allied front line.

D.H.9.												**29**
SINGLE-ENGINE AIRCRAFT				MULTI-ENGINE AIRCRAFT						PASS-ENGER	INSTRUCTOR/CLOUD FLYING (incl. in col. (1) to (10))	
DAY		NIGHT		DAY			NIGHT					
Dual	Pilot	Dual	Pilot	Dual	1st Pilot	2nd Pilot	Dual	1st Pilot	2nd Pilot		Dual	Pilot
(1)	(2)	(3)	(4)	(5)	(6)	(7)	(8)	(9)	(10)	(11)	(12)	(13)

Time off _ Time in air   Height   Course.

9·55 AM   2-40   11000′   Beauvais ±± – Flavy
                                – wheat field 3 miles
                                Inside British lines.

                              †
                         †   †
                    +   +
                      †   † (A.H.C)
                 (Lost)

                                ↖ ↖
                            ←   Attack

Personal memorabilia of Lt Alan Curtis preserved in the de Havilland Heritage Museum. Prize exhibit is the piece of tail fabric of D.H.9 C6114, in which he was shot down.

Lt Alan Curtis. During operations from November 1917 to July 1918, flying D.H.4s and D.H.9s, he attacked 32 targets in 43 missions, dropping 139 bombs with a total weight of 8,134 lb. Total operational flying time was 181 hours 55 minutes. This was much higher than the average life of a bomber pilot, indicating both great skill and luck.

A 'bombed-up' Liberty engined D.H.9A being prepared for flight with the aid of a Hucks starter.

Basically a D.H.9 with a 400 hp American Liberty 12 engine, the D.H.9A proved to be an outstanding strategic bomber in the closing months of the First World War. The Armistice caused plans to build 4,000 in America to be abandoned, but D.H.9As spearheaded Royal Air Force operations overseas throughout the 1920s.

A single bomb mounted beneath a D.H.9A converted by the Aircraft Disposal Company to have a Rolls-Royce Eagle VIII engine, cooled by prominent twin Lamblin radiators between the undercarriage legs. After this aircraft had been demonstrated in Madrid, similar D.H.9As were ordered for the Spanish Air Force.

This D.H.9, with a 250 hp Fiat A-12 engine, was built by Waring and Gillow, one of the furniture makers called in to boost production of the wooden warplanes of the First World War.

One of the 150 D.H.9As ordered from Mann Egerton. Altogether, thirteen companies built 'Nine-acks' in addition to the Westland Aircraft Works, which had been responsible for the original redesign and rebuild of a D.H.9 at its Yeovil factory.

When Germany began attacking targets in London and Eastern England with twin-engined bombers in 1917, the War Office realised that it had made a mistake in cancelling the D.H.3. Only eight of the 1,295 slightly larger D.H.10s that it ordered were delivered to the RAF before the Armistice. After the war, bombs gave way to air mail. D.H.10s of No. 120 Squadron operated daily mail services from Hawkinge to Cologne for the British Army of Occupation on the Rhine, one of them becoming the first aircraft to carry mail at night on 14 May 1919.

A mechanic servicing the port Liberty engine of a D.H.10 at Andover in 1918. When the bomber was ordered it was given the official name Amiens, the two prototypes becoming Amiens Mk I and Mk II, and production aircraft Amiens Mk IIIs.

Two

Age of Adventure

With the signing of the Armistice, contracts for military aircraft were cancelled, and Geoffrey de Havilland focussed his attention on the production of civilian aircraft. Initially, as might be expected, the early machines were adaptations of military types, the first step being to provide accommodation for passengers and freight. Thus the D.H.4 was fitted with a hinged lid on top of a cabin big enough for two facing passengers, providing what was described at the time as 'limousine comfort, entirely enclosed and free from wind or draught'.

The best remembered aircraft produced during the 1920s was the D.H.60 Moth. Seating two in comfort, strong enough for safe cross country flying and landings in open meadows, and powered after a time by a reliable Gipsy engine, it became a familiar sight on club airfields at home, in Europe and on those of the Empire abroad. Moths were used by such celebrities and pioneers as Alan Cobham, Amy Johnson, Francis Chichester and Jim Mollison.

The early 1930s saw the first flight of the D.H.82 Tiger Moth, destined to become one of the great trainers of all time and a firm favourite with flying clubs, right up to the present time. Also flown in the early 1930s was the D.H.84 Dragon, the first of a series of mini-airliners. It was followed by the four-engined D.H.86 and the twin-engined D.H.89 Dragon Rapide, which introduced economical air services throughout the world.

Previous pages: Lady passengers boarding this D.H.9, leased to the Dutch airline KLM by Aircraft Transport & Travel for a flight from Schiphol to London, were lent a leather coat, helmet, goggles, gloves – and a hot water bottle on really cold days.

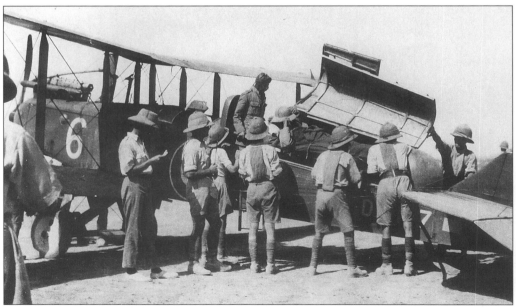

A converted D.H.9 being used as an air ambulance by the British Z Force in Somaliland, 1920. Pads on the backs of the ground crew were issued to protect the spinal column from overheating in the tropical climate.

The D.H.4A used to carry the first civilian international air mail from Britain to France was distinguished by a 'Royal Mail' pennant attached to the rudder.

Loading the first Paris-bound mailings on to the Aircraft Transport & Travel's D.H.4A at Hounslow aerodrome, 12 November 1919. The service cost 2s 6d per ounce.

D.H.4As, with an enclosed cabin seating two passengers face to face, offered slightly more comfort than A.T. & T.'s open-cockpit D.H.9s. This one is being prepared for flight at Hendon aerodrome in the summer of 1919.

The day bomber origins of the D.H.4R (R for racer) were barely discernible. It had been built in only ten days by a team of Airco enthusiasts, who installed a 450 hp Napier Lion engine with a large chin radiator, shortened the lower wings and covered the rear cockpit. Flown by Capt G.W. Gathergood, a company test pilot, it won the Victory Aerial Derby on 21 June 1919, covering two laps of a 94.5 mile course around London at 129.34 mph.

Powered by an improved version of the Napier Lion engine, C6078, the D.H.9 testbeds, set a new height record of 30,500 ft on 2 January 1919. Lieutenant A.W. Blowes (bottom left), in the rear cockpit, collapsed through failure of his oxygen supply; the engine stopped at 30,500 ft; during descent the aircraft became uncontrollable for a time at 27,000 ft. Back at 20,000 ft Blowes regained consciousness but both he and the pilot, Captain Andrew Lang (top), landed with a frostbitten face, fingers and toes.

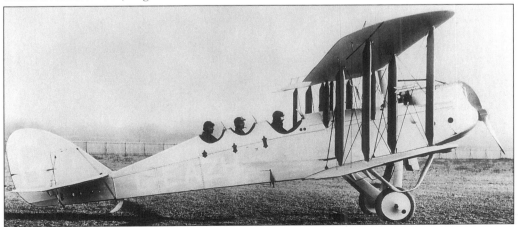

One of two D.H.9s converted to have three tandem open cockpits by the Aircraft Disposal Company in 1922 for Ad Astra Aero of Zürich.

To improve passenger comfort, a light wood and canvas cover was devised to convert the rear cockpit into a cabin for two facing persons in the D.H.9C. The wings were swept back slightly to compensate for the rearward movement of the centre of gravity.

The D.H.10 civil mailplane G-EAJO, with two Liberty engines, was operated by Aircraft Transport & Travel in 1919.

Many D.H.4s and D.H.9s were used to pioneer air routes overseas. Here the crew of a D.H.4 sign for the mail on an early Qantas flight in Australia.

Line-up of D.H.9B and 9C aircraft at Stag Lane in 1922. They formed part of the de Havilland Aeroplane Hire Service fleet, which was in great demand by companies taking air photographs, newspaper reporters and wealthy people in a hurry. It also gave the company's designers valuable feedback on commercial flying.

Basically a D.H.9A with a fuselage widened to seat four passengers in pairs, the D.H.16 was Airco's first purely civil type. Entry to the cabin was by means of a ladder and hinged roof.

Captain H. 'Jerry' Shaw was pilot of the first KLM passenger flight between Croydon Airport and Amsterdam in a D.H.16 leased from A.T. & T, on 17 May 1920.

The first flight by the Dutch national airline KLM from Croydon to Amsterdam carried a cargo of two journalists, a bundle of newspapers and a message from the Lord Mayor of London.

A D.H.16 being prepared for flight at Schiphol aerodrome in the 1920s. Bad weather or technical problems often forced pilots to make intermediate landings, and a flight between Amsterdam and London could take up to forty hours – very different from the one hour journey that is now routine.

Passengers boarding a D.H.18 of Instone Air Line, under the watchful eye of a policeman. G-EAUF was named *City of Paris*.

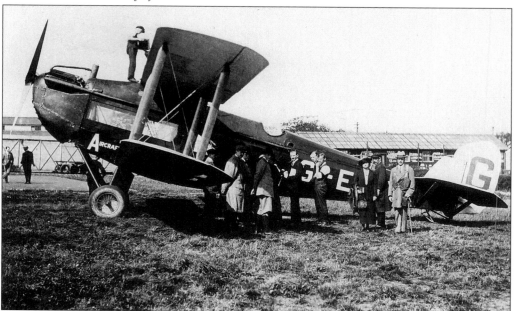

The D.H.18 had a proper cabin for its eight passengers. The pilot continued to occupy an open cockpit, as it was considered unsafe for him to be enclosed at that period. The precarious method of refuelling is noteworthy.

Although the relationship was barely recognisable, the Handley Page H.P.20 slotted-wing research aircraft, built at Cricklewood in 1921, used the fuselage, undercarriage and tail unit of a Westland-built D.H.9A. It landed at only 43 mph.

Named *City of New York*, G-EBBT was Instone's second D.H.34. On this type the pilot was now seated forward of the wings, but still in an open cockpit. One of Daimler's D.H.34s, G-EBBS, was the first airliner to make two round trips between Croydon and le Bourget, Paris, in one day.

Compared with other airliners of the early 1920s, the D.H.34 accommodated its passengers in considerable comfort. On Daimler aircraft a cabin boy served refreshments in flight.

To speed help to aircraft stranded overseas through engine failure, Daimler could carry a spare Napier Lion in their D.H.34s. As the engines were too long to fit inside the cabin, the propeller shaft projected through a hole in the side – normally covered by a fabric patch.

Daimler Hire's first D.H.34, G-EBBQ, made its inaugural flight to Paris on 2 April 1922, carrying newspapers, only seven days after its first test flight by Alan Cobham.

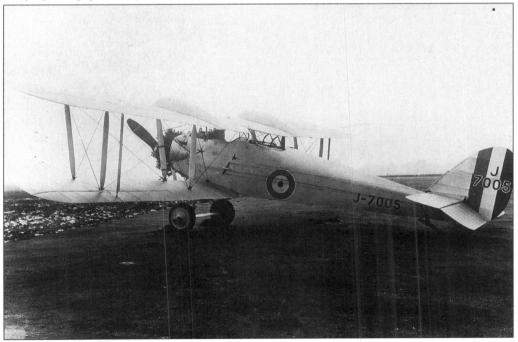

Built in 1923 as a high-performance two-seat reconnaissance fighter, the little known D.H.42 Dormouse was armed with two forward-firing machine guns and another in the rear cockpit. A large oval cutout in the top wing centre-section gave the pilot a good view upward. The only Dormouse flown was used for a time by the Wireless and Photographic Flight of the Royal Aircraft Establishment at Farnborough.

Passengers about to board a D.H.50, a four-seater designed to replace the D.H.9Cs of the de Havilland Hire Service. The type was used extensively overseas and in Australia was regarded as the first successful passenger aircraft.

First aircraft of the D.H.50 series to enter commercial service in the British Empire overseas was G-AUER, a D.H.50A with a larger radiator. After use by Qantas, it was named *Victory* and became the first aeroplane used by Australia's famous Flying Doctor service.

During its time with Qantas, G-AUER carried S.M. Bruce, the Australian Prime Minister, during his electioneering campaign in Queensland in 1924. To the right is a D.H.9C which the D.H.50 replaced.

Hippomenes, the last of three D.H.50Js, with a 385 hp Jaguar engine, built by Qantas at Longreach. During later use by Pacific Air Transport in New Guinea it flew 1,200 miles in one day in 1935, making fifteen round trips between Lae and Wau.

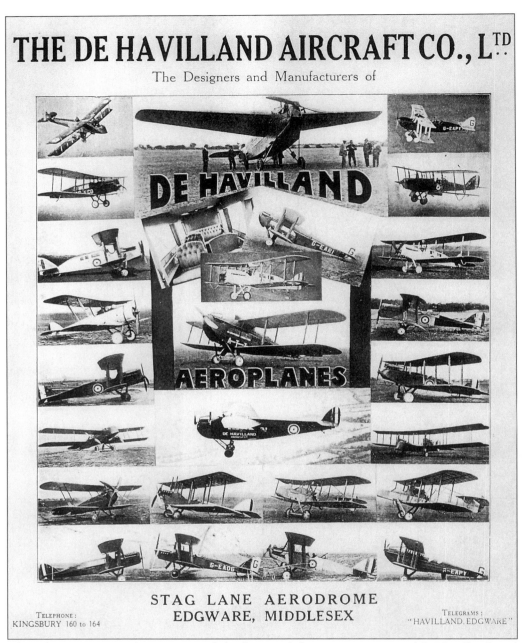

THE DE HAVILLAND AIRCRAFT CO., L.^{TD}

The Designers and Manufacturers of

DE HAVILLAND

AEROPLANES

STAG LANE AERODROME
EDGWARE, MIDDLESEX

This advertisement in the magazine *Flight* illustrated the extensive range of de Havilland civil and military aircraft that had been designed and built by the late 1920s.

Alan Cobham (pilot), B.W.G. Emmott (photographer) and A.B. Elliott (mechanic) with the Jaguar-engined D.H.50J in which they made a survey flight to Cape Town between November 1925 and March 1926. In the middle of 1926 Cobham and Elliott flew to Melbourne and back. During the return flight Elliott was killed by a stray bullet fired by a Bedouin between Baghdad and Basra.

As much of the survey flight to Australia was over water, Cobham's D.H.50J was fitted with floats by Short Brothers at Rochester. When the aircraft returned to England it landed on the Thames at Westminster, in front of the Houses of Parliament.

The record breaking D.H.50J on parade through London. By the time the aircraft landed on the Thames its Empire route proving and survey flights on behalf of Imperial Airways totalled 62,000 miles.

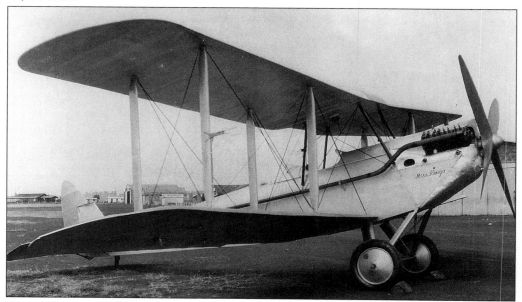

One of the three D.H.51 inexpensive 'practical touring' aircraft built in 1925, with war-surplus 90 hp R.A.F.1A engines costing 14s 6d each. *Miss Kenya* was used extensively in primitive conditions in that country and, in September 1928, became G-KAA, the first aircraft on the Kenyan register. It is now back in Britain with its originally allotted registration G-EBIR.

Two D.H.52 gliders were entered for the *Daily Mail* £1,000 Gliding Competition in 1922. Unusual design features included the use of scooter wheels, and leather hinges for the elevators, of the type found on old wooden clothes horses, to allow 90 degrees of upward and downward movement. Flight trials were unsatisfactory and the gliders were scrapped.

Second prototype of the D.H.53 Humming Bird single-seat monoplane built for the *Daily Mail* light aeroplane trials at Lympne in 1923. The D.H.53 was the first true light aircraft built by de Havilland; one of them covered 59.3 miles on one gallon of fuel.

Capt Geoffrey de Havilland and an early D.H.60 Moth, a scaled-down development of the D.H.51. The robust construction and pleasant flying qualities of the small two-seater initiated the birth of the worldwide flying club movement in the mid-1920s.

The prototype Moth, G-EBKT, was first flown by Geoffrey de Havilland on 22 February 1925. Shown here with the second prototype, it made headlines when Alan Cobham flew it 1,000 miles from Croydon to Zürich and back in one day on 29 May 1925.

When production of Moths at Stag Lane increased to about one aircraft a day in 1926, it was clear that the supply of war-surplus Renault parts for the Cirrus engines would soon be exhausted. Frank Halford designed the all-new 100 hp Gipsy engine specially for this D.H.60G version, and Moth deliveries were able to reach sixteen a week by 1929.

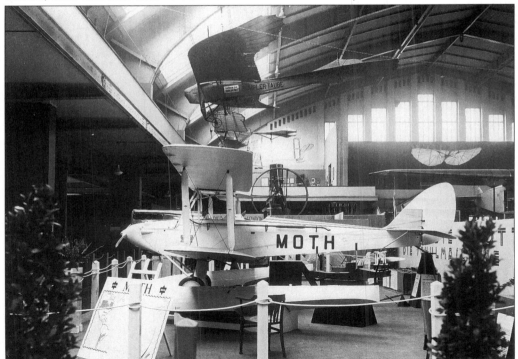

Moths could be fitted with floats for operation in places like Canada and parts of Africa, where lakes offered better landing sites than the rough surrounding country. The little two-seaters were so popular worldwide that this one easily justified its display among historic aircraft in Germany.

G-AADX was one of a batch of Coupé Gipsy Moths delivered in 1928. They did not prove popular because the weight of the Triplex-glazed canopy reduced the payload by 25 lb.

With its wings folded, the Moth could be towed behind a family car. By 1929, eighty-five per cent of all privately-owned aircraft on the British register were Moths.

With welded steel tubing instead of wood for its fuselage structure, the D.H.60M Moth was designed primarily for export. HRH The Prince of Wales (left) took delivery of G-AALG in which he flew with a Royal safety pilot.

The oldest Moth still maintained in flying condition is G-EBLV, the eighth of the original Cirrus-engined D.H.60s. First delivered by Alan Cobham to the Lancashire Aero Club at Woodford on 29 August 1925, it was rebuilt by de Havilland apprentices in 1951 and is now with the Shuttleworth Collection at Old Warden Aerodrome, Bedfordshire.

Publicity photograph intended to suggest that flying and planning long distance flights in the reliable Gipsy Moth was an easy matter. All that was needed was a globe and map – even for girls – a situation that belied the careful planning and preparation required when Amy Johnson flew solo from England to Australia in Gipsy Moth G-AAAH *Jason,* now in the Science Museum in London.

A familiar sight in the early 1930s. AA patrol men, specially trained in the handling of aircraft, were to be seen at all major air meetings.

Flown by Geoffrey de Havilland as his personal aircraft, the appropriately-registered G-AAAA Gipsy Moth is seen here dropping a message to an AA patrolman in an age before private aircraft were fitted with radio.

With the opening of the underground railway station at Edgware, the district quickly became a dormitory suburb for Londoners. The encroachment of local housing is evident from this view of the Stag Lane factory, taken just before de Havilland acquired its new 'green field' site at Hatfield in 1930.

The de Havilland site at Hatfield in 1930. First to move there was the de Havilland School of Flying. By the end of 1932 the entire airframe factory had been transferred from Stag Lane.

Within a few months of moving to Hatfield, de Havilland had built a new club house, swimming pool and hangars, and had begun erecting new workshops (right background).

The large engineering workshops and imposing design office block under construction in the early 1930s. Within that decade, Hatfield would deliver a superb succession of Moth and Tiger Moth trainers; Leopard and Hornet Moth tourers; Dragon, D.H.86 and Rapide light transports and the very modern Albatross and Flamingo monoplane airliners.

A D.H.60G Gipsy Moth at Wynberg Aerodrome, Cape Town. The reliability of its engine contributed greatly to the Moth's popularity in the vast territory of South Africa.

Safely behind a barrier, trainees are shown how to start the engine of a Gipsy Moth by swinging the propeller. Noteworthy are the large chocks both in front of and behind the wheels and the fire equipment by the port wing.

The D.H.61 Giant Moth of 1927 was designed as a D.H.50J replacement; ten were built, mostly for service in Australia, New Guinea and Canada. To ensure an adequate view past the wide six-to-ten-seat cabin, the cockpit was raised above the top of the fuselage, the pilot being protected by a long streamlined fairing.

The second Giant Moth, G-CAJT, was fitted with floats at Short's Rochester works and test flown in June 1928. It was one of two D.H.61s fitted with floats for operation by firefighters from the many lakes and rivers in Canada.

Seventeen bags of air mail were carried from Brisbane to Darwin by Giant Moth VH-UJB *Apollo* on 25 April 1931, as one leg of the first official air mail run from Australia to Britain.

The fastest two-seat aeroplane in the world when first flown, in 1926, the D.H.65 Hound was intended to demonstrate what could be achieved if designers were not hampered by official specifications. Although it set records of up to 162 mph, carrying a 2,204 lb load, the Air Ministry bitterly disappointed de Havilland by rejecting it.

D.H.66 Hercules *City of Baghdad*, one of the Imperial Airways fleet that eventually extended the Desert Air Mail route all the way from Cairo to Delhi. Specially designed for operation in tropical regions, the D.H.66 had three engines to reduce the possibility of forced landings in hazardous areas.

D.H.66 Hercules seven-to-fourteen-seat airliner landing at Wingfield aerodrome, Cape Town, South Africa, piloted by Sir Alan Cobham on 1 December 1932. With the Afrikaans name *Stad van Kaapstad* on one side of its nose and the English *City of Cape Town* on the other, it was bought by Cobham for his National Aviation Day air circus which toured Britain from 1931 to 1935, giving flying displays and five shilling joyrides to create an airminded public.

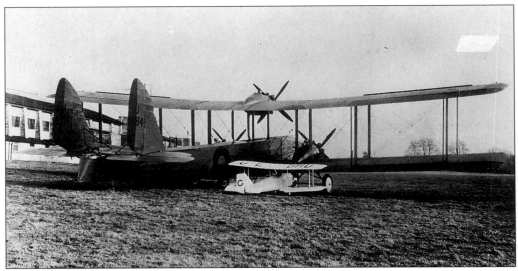

Impressed by the reliability of the D.H.66, the Air Ministry ordered the D.H.72 prototype as a possible replacement for the Vickers Virginia night bomber. The centre engine was moved to the top wing when the Ministry requested a machine gun in the nose. A single D.H.72 was completed in 1931 by the Gloster Aircraft Company, explaining the diminutive Gloster Gannet in the foreground to emphasise its size.

Air Ministry Specification F.20/27 called for a completely new kind of interceptor, able to climb fast enough to eliminate the need for standing patrols, with sufficient fuel for only a quick attack, and without radio to save weight. The de Havilland Company's response, the D.H.77, with a maximum speed of 204 mph, offered performance comparable with that of biplane competitors that had engines 40 per cent more powerful. No production contract was obtained, however, as the Air Ministry was not ready to trust the safety of a monoplane in 1929.

With the D.H.80A Puss Moth, de Havilland lightplanes changed to a monoplane configuration, an enclosed cabin for the pilot and two passengers, and a steel tube fuselage as standard. The result was 22 per cent faster than a Moth with a similar 120 hp Gipsy engine. Pilots like Jim and Amy (Johnson) Mollison set many records in Puss Moths in the 1930s. This one, named *Springbok*, was photographed at Wynberg aerodrome, Cape Town.

A 1930s newsreel item titled *Speed in Three Elements* featured a dramatic race sequence between an LNER express train, a speed boat and a Puss Moth. Needless to say, the de Havilland aircraft won!

Built by de Havilland to the design of Don Juan de la Cierva, whose company supplied the rotor head, was the Cierva C.24 Autogiro, first flown in September 1931. With a two-seat steel tube fuselage similar in construction to that of a Puss Moth, a tricycle undercarriage and Gipsy engine, it was used by Cierva for a tour of Europe and is now displayed in the de Havilland Heritage Centre.

D.H.82 Tiger Moth flying over the Needles rock formation, Isle of Wight. First flown in 1931, more than 9,000 Tiger Moths were built during the next fourteen years, becoming the principal elementary trainers for Britain and the Empire during the Second World War.

First to bear the name Tiger Moth, the D.H.71 high-speed research monoplane was used as an advertising medium outside the new Hatfield factory at the time of the 1933 King's Cup Air Race. It had set a 100 km closed-circuit world speed record of 186.47 mph on 24 August 1927.

Two Tiger Moths at Jodhpur, India, one of the twenty-five countries to which the trainer was exported.

Tiger Moths in service with the Royal Rhodesian Air Force.

D.H.82B Queen Bee radio-controlled aircraft being launched at sea by catapult, as a target for Naval gunners. Although externally similar to the Tiger Moth, the Queen Bee combined a Gipsy Moth wooden fuselage, for cheapness and buoyancy, with Tiger Moth wings and a Gipsy Major engine. Over 400 Queen Bees were built.

The fine handling qualities of the Tiger Moth are exemplified in this top view of one, taken from a second Tiger flying inverted in a 'mirror' formation. Pilot of the top aircraft was Bob Winter ('Archbishop' of the Tiger Club), whose face can be seen above G-AOAA, flown by Bill Innes ('The Deacon').

The D.H.83 Fox Moth of 1932 used Tiger Moth wings and a new fuselage accommodating four passengers in an enclosed cabin, to become what was described as 'the first British aeroplane able to support itself financially in the air'. Because of this, Fox Moths pioneered air travel in many parts of the British Empire.

Fox Moth G-ABUT, winner of the 1932 King's Cup race at an average speed of 124.13 mph. This was pilot Wally Hope's third win in this prestigious event.

Designed as a 'twin-engined Fox Moth' to provide a London to Paris service at low fares, the D.H.84 Dragon carried between six and eight passengers at a cruising speed of 109 mph, for an hourly consumption of only 13 gallons of fuel. Eight Dragon 2s of Jersey Airways flew 19,761 passengers between Heston, the island's beaches and Paris during 1934.

Photographs of the coronation of King George VI, in May 1937, being put on board a Dragon of Railway Air Services at Croydon Airport for rapid transportation to the *Belfast Evening Telegraph* in Northern Ireland.

Dragon G-ACCV *Seafarer* was ferried to the USA by Jim and Amy Mollison in 1933 for an attempt on the world distance record. It crashed at Bridgeport, Connecticut, on the way to New York, from where they had planned to fly non-stop to Baghdad. The engines and the special fuel tanks were salvaged and built into a replacement Dragon, G-ACJM *Seafarer II*, but this failed to take off with a full fuel load. It was renamed *Trail of the Caribou* for a third attempt by J.R. Ayling (left) and Leonard Reid in 1934, when excessive fuel consumption forced them to land prematurely at Heston. This was, however, the first non-stop flight from the mainland of Canada to Britain.

Privately modified Dragon for air ambulance duties in South Africa. The small round windows reduced the temperature in the 'medical' cabin.

The faster, more comfortable D.H.89 Dragon Rapide attracted many overseas operators such as Tata Air Lines of India, one of whose aircraft is shown here. The small airline grew into Air India, managed by its founder J.R.D. Tata, who had begun with a single Puss Moth in 1932.

Three refurbished ex-military D.H.89 Dragon Rapides and a Percival Proctor leaving the de Havilland Repair Unit at Witney, Oxfordshire, after the Second World War. They were on their way to Lisbon, Portugal, for service with the new airline Companhia de Transportes Aereos.

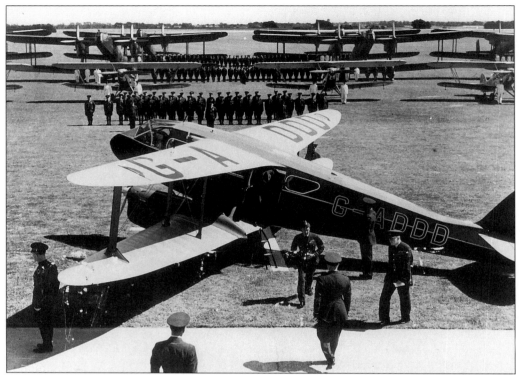

A Dragon Rapide of the King's Flight carried HM King Edward VIII on his first visit to the Royal Air Force after his accession. Accompanied by his brother, the Duke of York, he visited Mildenhall on 8 July 1936 and three other Air Force stations. In the last six months of 1936 the Rapide was used for 61 Royal flights.

The first four-engined de Havilland aeroplane, the prototype D.H.86, was designed and built in four months to meet an Australian requirement for a ten-seat airliner able to fly safely across the Java and Timor Seas. This one made the first-ever aerial delivery of tyres to Jersey from Goodyear's Southampton depot in March 1935.

Inbound from Paris, the passengers from this D.H.86 are about to use the new mobile walkway at Gatwick, to where airline activities were transferred from Heston in June 1936.

The adventure of flying in the mid-1930s is epitomised in this greeting card depicting a Gipsy Moth, Dragon Rapide, and with vintage Rolls-Royce and Austin Seven cars.

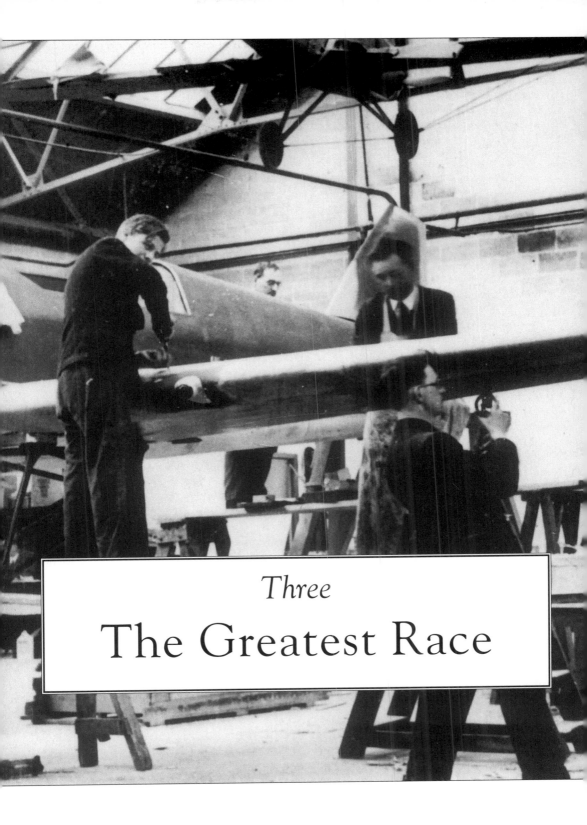

Three
The Greatest Race

Sixty-four aircraft were entered for the MacRobertson England-to-Australia International Air Race organised to commemorate the centenary of the founding of the State of Victoria. Many dropped out as the date set for the race approached, but on the day, 20 October 1934, a total of twenty-four aircraft took off from Mildenhall.

Among them were three two-seat D.H.88 Comets, specially designed for the race by de Havilland, whose directors were determined that the winner of this prestigious contest must be British. Although each of the Comet's Gipsy Six R engines gave only 230 hp, the aircraft combined a good take-off performance with high speed and a range of nearly 3,000 miles, obtained by a good combination of careful streamlining, a thin wing, flaps, retractable undercarriage and variable-pitch propellers.

Each Comet was painted in distinctive racing colours. The Mollisons' *Black Magic*, G-ACSP, was black and gold; G-ACSR, flown by Owen Cathcart-Jones and Ken Waller, was green; G-ACSS, named *Grosvenor House* and flown by C.W.A. Scott and Tom Campbell Black, was a brilliant scarlet with a white flash.

Jim and Amy Mollison had to retire at Allahabad after their aircraft was inadvertently refuelled with commercial motor spirit. Fierce determination enabled Scott and Black to overcome fatigue and to land first in Melbourne in an elapsed time of 70 hours, 54 minutes and 18 seconds. Cathcart-Jones and Waller were fourth, in a time of just over 108 hours.

Two more Comets were built after the race and all five were used for record-breaking flights around Europe and to countries of the Empire. The most exciting exploits were those of the Australia race winner, G-ACSS. One planned venture that did not materialise was to use it as a bomber to assassinate Hitler during a Nazi parade in Berlin.

Previous pages: One of the first Comets built for the England-Australia Race taking shape in secrecy at the Stag Lane factory, where a D.H.71 was temporarily relegated to the roof rafters. Final assembly and test flying were done at Hatfield.

Comet G-ACSR, flown by Owen Cathcart-Jones and Ken Waller, undergoing urgent repairs after landing with the undercarriage only partially lowered. The repairs were completed just twelve hours before the start of the race.

Their Majesties King George V and Queen Mary visiting Mildenhall in October 1934. To the right of the picture are Jim and Amy Mollison, in front of their black-painted *Black Magic*. So urgent was work on the Comet that special permission was given for the de Havilland engineers to continue the final preparations while the Royal party toured the competing aircraft.

The Mollisons' Comet, G-ACSP *Black Magic*, at the start of the race, at Mildenhall as dawn broke on 20 October 1934. This crew and aircraft, great favourites with the British people, retired at Allahabad where the engines were damaged after refuelling with commercial motor spirit.

Owen Cathcart-Jones and Ken Waller took time for a photograph while their Comet was being refuelled at Allahabad. G-ACSR came fourth in the race after a flight taking just over 108 hours, including a rest at Mount Isa, Queensland.

Piloted by Charles Scott and Tom Campbell Black, Comet G-ACSS arrives in Melbourne, Australia, to win the speed prize after a flight of 11,333 miles in 70 hours 54 minutes. The second aircraft to arrive was a DC-2 of KLM after a flight of 90 hours 13 minutes; third was a Boeing 247D in 92 hours.

After winning the race, Comet G-ACSS returned to Britain by sea, as deck cargo. Here the fully assembled aircraft is about to be hoisted on board the ship for the homeward journey from Melbourne.

The fifth and final Comet, G-ADEF, being named *Boomerang* during the handover ceremony at Hatfield in August 1935. Intended for attempts on major long distance records, the aircraft experienced engine problems over the Sudan during an attempt on the London-to-Cape Town record, causing the crew to abandon the aircraft by parachute.

Back home in Britain, G-ACSS was taken over by the Air Ministry for trials at the Aircraft and Armament Experimental Establishment, Martlesham Heath. Now identified as K5084, it was damaged when the undercarriage failed to lock down on 30 August 1935. After repair, the Comet was flown in the RAF Display at Hendon on 27 June 1936.

Comet K5084, formerly G-ACSS, shows off its distinctive tapered wings which made landings tricky, during the RAF Display.

To commemorate the achievements of the D.H.88 Comet, a hotel bearing its name was opened in Hatfield, near the de Havilland factory, in 1937. The hotel is of roughly aeroplane shape in plan view and was enhanced by a model of G-ACSS, with a wing span of eight feet, on a decorated stone pillar. The hotel and model remain local landmarks today.

During tests on 2 September 1936 the landing gear of K5084 collapsed. The severe damage resulted in the Comet being declared a 'write-off' and it was put up for sale as scrap. Fortunately, the aircraft was acquired by F.E. Tasker and rebuilt by Essex Aero of Gravesend, who fitted new engines and propellers. After it had been painted pale blue and renamed *The Orphan*, G-ACSS finished fourth in the 1937 Marseilles-Damascus-Paris race.

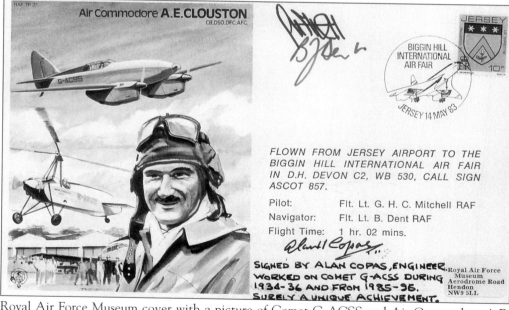

Royal Air Force Museum cover with a picture of Comet G-ACSS and Air Commodore A.E. Clouston, pilot of the aircraft in the 1937 Marseilles-Damascus-Paris race. The cover is signed by de Havilland design engineer Alan Copas, who had the unique experience of helping to build the aircraft in 1934 and then working on the same aircraft during its restoration and exhibition between 1985 and 1996.

Comet G-ACSS, then named *The Burberry*, at Croydon Airport in November 1937 as Clouston and Mrs Kirby Green prepared to take off in an attempt to break the England-to-Cape Town and return record. They reduced it to 15 days and 17 hours. After one last record-breaking flight to New Zealand the aircraft returned to Gravesend, where it remained during the Second World War until it was restored to *Grosvenor House* splendour for display at the 1951 Festival of Britain exhibition.

The partially restored D.H.88 Comet racer G-ACSS, winner of the 1934 England-to-Australia Air Race, beside its later namesake, a D.H.106 Comet jet airliner, prior to the Festival of Britain exhibition in 1951. Now restored to flying condition, the aircraft currently forms part of the Shuttleworth Collection based at Old Warden Aerodrome, Bedfordshire.

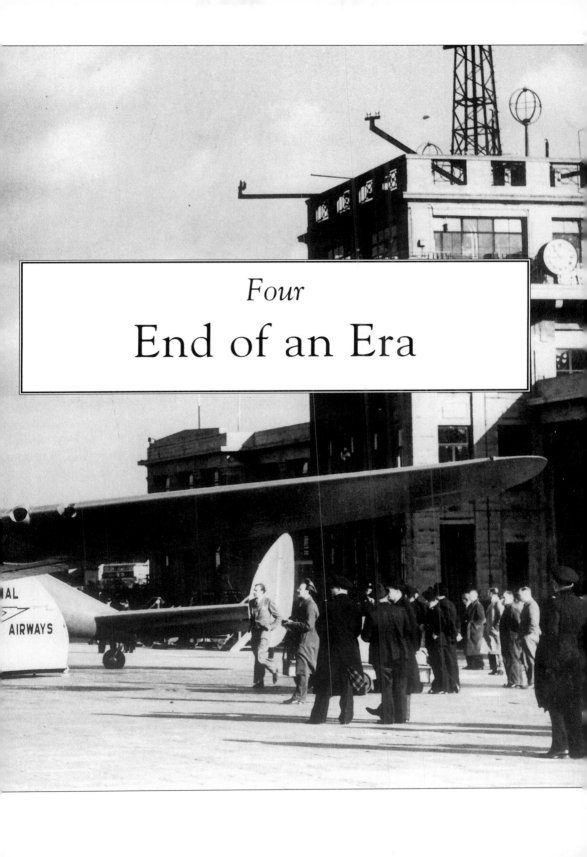

Four

End of an Era

The aircraft that took second place in The Greatest Race to reach Melbourne was the Douglas DC-2, entered by KLM. This caused some sobering thought at de Havilland. Their Comet, specially designed for racing, had only just beaten a large American airliner that was in commercial service, earning money.

To enable Britain to compete against such aircraft on the airline routes, de Havilland designed a 200 mph, four-engined passenger monoplane. To assist the project, the Air Ministry placed a contract for two experimental Transatlantic mailplane versions with extra fuel tanks. The result was the finely streamlined D.H.91 Albatross, considered by many people to be the most beautiful of all the aeroplanes of the 1930s. Britain's national airline, Imperial Airways, ordered five, each with seats for twenty-two passengers.

The Albatross was soon followed by the twin-engined D.H.95 Flamingo, the first stressed-skin, all-metal aircraft built by the company. The maximum speed of the Flamingo was higher than that of the Comet racer, a performance which attracted official interest.

Both the Albatross and the Flamingo were impressed into military service. The Albatross operated on the shuttle service to Lisbon and made courier flights to Egypt and India, while camouflaged Flamingoes were operated by British Overseas Airways Corporation in the Near East as its 'K' class of airliners. Although the war prevented these two advanced transports from displaying their full potential, they pointed the way to airliners that would open up a whole new world of high-speed air travel after the war had been won.

Previous pages: D.H.91 Albatross *Frobisher* of Imperial Airways on the apron beside the control tower at Croydon Airport, perhaps the most photographed building in aviation history. A Douglas DC-2 is approaching to land.

The prototype of the all-wood D.H.91 Albatross nearing completion at Hatfield in 1937. The close cowlings of the 525 hp Gipsy Twelve engines contributed significantly to the fine lines of this high-speed airliner.

The prototype Albatross, E-2/G-AEVV, was one of two Transatlantic mailplane versions ordered by the Air Ministry. This photograph of preparations for its first flight, on 20 May 1937, shows the tall inset fins and rudders fitted initially.

The Albatross is considered by many to have been the most beautiful of all de Havilland aeroplanes, even including the D.H.106 Comet jet airliner of a later generation.

Albatross G-AFDI *Frobisher*, flagship of the Imperial Airways fleet of 'F' class airliners. The passenger versions, which had additional cabin windows, averaged 219 mph on their first experimental Christmas mail deliveries to Cairo in December 1938. Passenger services to Paris, Brussels and Zürich had to end with the outbreak of the Second World War when the Albatross fleet was camouflaged for official duties. *Frobisher* was destroyed during a German air raid on Whitchurch on 20 December 1940.

The spacious four-abreast twenty-two passenger cabin of Albatross G-AFDI *Frobisher* set new standards of comfort.

Railway Air Services' D.H.86B *Venus* embarking passengers at Croydon Airport in 1938, with Imperial Airways Albatross *Fiona* in the background.

Albatross G-AFDK *Fortuna* after crashing on the mudflats near Shannon in July 1943. This aircraft, with the other Albatrosses, had been impressed into Government service at the outbreak of war, camouflaged, and then used, among other duties, on courier services to Portugal, Egypt and India.

Stamps issued to commemorate the fiftieth anniversary of the opening of Guernsey Airport in 1939. Regular services to London, Southampton, Exeter and Shoreham were operated by Guernsey Airways, using fourteen-seat D.H.86 Express airliners depicted on the stamps. Many other de Havilland aircraft have been featured on postage stamps all over the world.

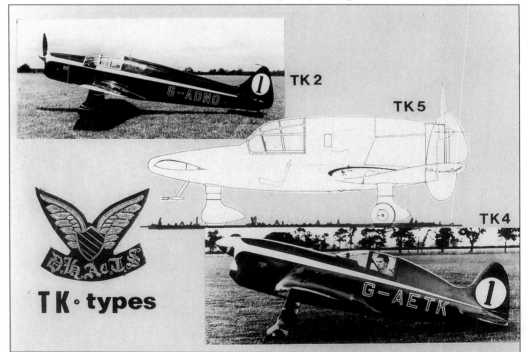

Three of the five 'TK' aircraft built by students of the de Havilland Technical School in the 1930s. The TK5 was a single-seat research aircraft. During trials it refused to leave the ground and was scrapped.

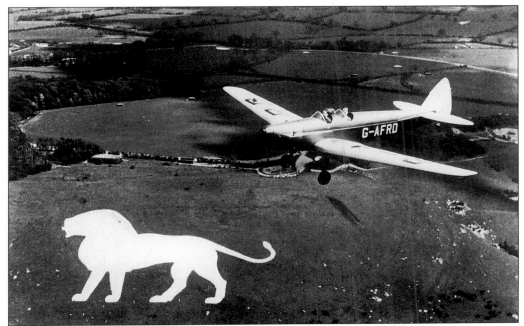

A D.H.94 Moth Minor of 1937 flying over the well known chalk lion of Whipsnade, not far from Hatfield. Designed as a monoplane successor to the Moth, the D.H.94 was easier to build and maintain, and provided improved performance with a Gipsy Minor engine of only 80 hp.

The D.H.95 Flamingo twelve-to-eighteen passenger airliner of 1938 was the first de Havilland aircraft of all-metal stressed-skin construction.

Flamingo cockpit. The excellent field of view was much appreciated by pilots accustomed often to peering through 'letterbox' windows.

Comfort in the 1930s: reclining seats in the cabin of a Flamingo.

A Flamingo about to take off in wintry conditions.

A Flamingo in the black and silver livery of British Air Transport in 1952. This aircraft had first flown in 1940, when it was impressed by the Admiralty into Fleet Air Arm service with the name *Merlin VI*. Based at Donibristle, it operated to the Orkneys, Shetlands and Northern Ireland. It was the only Flamingo to be used on commercial services after the war.

The inevitability of war had been apparent long before it began in September 1939. To meet the needs of the worsening situation, de Havilland studied the possibilities of a bomber version of the Albatross. Far more attractive was the concept of a truly fast bomber – so fast that no defensive armament would be required. Construction could be of wood to take advantage of the company's experience of using this material, with the added advantage that it would not make demands upon scarce metals needed for other aircraft. The final design was for a relatively small, twin-engined aeroplane carrying 1,000 lb of bombs 1,500 miles.

Official interest was at best lukewarm, but finally a contract was placed for fifty of the new bombers. The end result was the legendary D.H.98 Mosquito, one of the most remarkable warplanes produced by any nation during the Second World War. Early flight trials showed it to be faster than any other combat aircraft in the world.

Mosquitoes perfected the technique of attacking selected targets with an accuracy not equalled until the advent of 'smart' laser-guided bombs in the 1990s. By 1944 Mosquitoes were carrying a greater bomb load than some large four-engined bombers, which needed crews of up to eleven men plus escorting fighters. Pathfinder Mosquitoes marked city targets with coloured flares while Mosquitoes with cannon, machine guns, six-pounder guns and bombs attacked aircraft, shipping and submarines.

The war period saw the maiden flight, on 20 September 1943, of the first de Havilland jet-propelled aircraft, the D.H.100 Vampire fighter powered by a Goblin turbojet, also designed and made by the company. Production aircraft had a top speed above 500 mph.

During the war de Havilland produced 11,540 aircraft, of which 5,599 were made at Hatfield.

Previous pages: The distinctive 1930s style Design Office block at Hatfield in its wartime camouflage. The barbed wire in the foreground was intended to deter saboteurs.

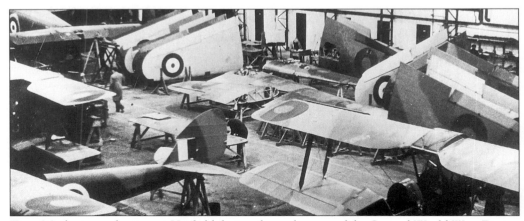

Tiger Moths in production at Hatfield during the early years of the Second World War. During this period, the last of the Flamingoes were completed and repair of Hawker Hurricane wings undertaken.

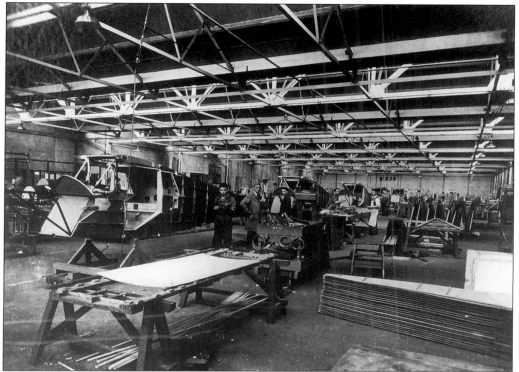

D.H.87 Hornet Moths being built alongside the Tiger Moth line. Of 165 of these side-by-side, two-seat cabin biplanes that were built, many were used for official wartime duties.

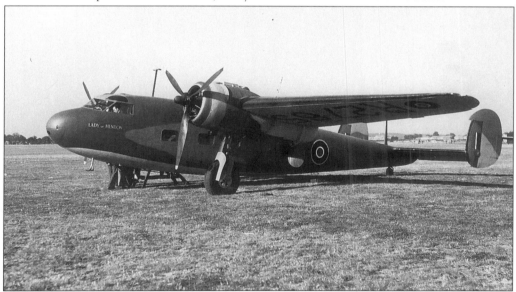

Following the outbreak of war Flamingoes were used by VIPs, including Prime Minister Winston Churchill, when making urgent visits to France during the pre-Dunkirk period. *Lady of Hendon*, first flown in February 1940, served with No. 24 Squadron, RAF. Another was allocated to possible emergency use by the Royal Family.

Hatfield at war – 1. To prevent surprise landings by enemy aircraft, old cars, minus their engines, were placed across the airfield at night.

Hatfield at war – 2. Dummy windows were painted on the doors of the hangar (left) and three dummy chimneys added to the roof to confuse low-flying enemy bombers.

Hatfield at war – 3. The damaged Sheet Metal Building ('94 shop) after four bombs were dropped on the airfield by a Junkers Ju 88 on 3 October 1940. The raid killed twenty-one people, injured seventy and destroyed 80 per cent of the Mosquito work in progress. The German bomber was damaged by gunfire from the site and crashed soon afterwards at nearby Hertingfordbury.

Hatfield at war – 4. A Tiger Moth being 'bombed up' at Hatfield during anti-invasion preparations in 1940. About 1,500 sets of bomb racks were produced for aircraft at flying schools, together with operational instructions. Trials were completed satisfactorily over the airfield at Hatfield but no bombs were dropped in combat.

Salisbury Hall, in a wooded area close to Hatfield, was where the D.H.98 Mosquito was designed in 1940. The first prototype was constructed in a hangar near the house, followed by four more aircraft. This site was also used for the construction of the first two Horsa gliders.

Mosquito mockup at Salisbury Hall in early 1940.

The prototype Mosquito, E-0234/W4050, after its short journey by road from Salisbury Hall to Hatfield where it was reassembled for engine runs and its first flight, piloted by Geoffrey de Havilland Jr, on 25 November 1940. On the ground, tarpaulins were used for camouflage and a blast wall provided both screening and some protection against air attack. In the air, the Mosquito confounded Air Ministry 'experts' who had seen no future for an unarmed wooden warplane.

The second prototype of the Mosquito, W4052, the night fighter version, being readied for its first flight. To avoid the loss of a month through dismantling and re-erection, the aircraft was flown from a field adjacent to Salisbury Hall that was in the process of being ploughed up by a local farmer.

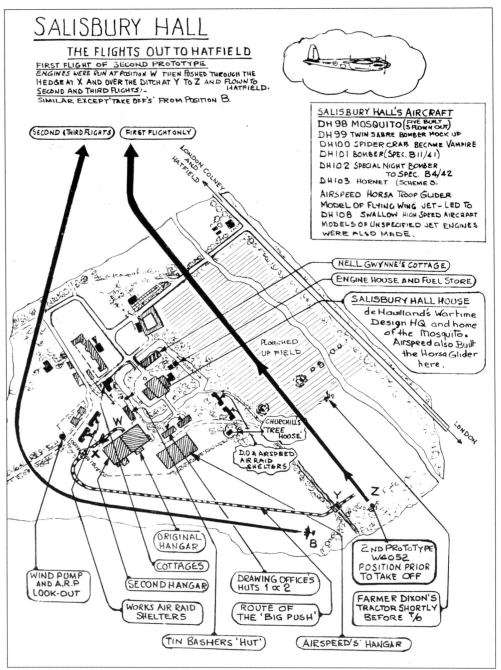

SALISBURY HALL

THE FLIGHTS OUT TO HATFIELD

FIRST FLIGHT OF SECOND PROTOTYPE
ENGINES WERE RUN AT POSITION W THEN PUSHED THROUGH THE
HEDGE AT X AND OVER THE DITCH AT Y TO Z AND FLOWN TO
SECOND AND THIRD FLIGHTS:- HATFIELD.
SIMILAR EXCEPT 'TAKE OFF'S' FROM POSITION B.

SECOND & THIRD FLIGHTS   FIRST FLIGHT ONLY

LONDON COLNEY AND HATFIELD

SALISBURY HALL'S AIRCRAFT
DH 98 MOSQUITO (FIVE BUILT 3 FLOWN OUT)
DH 99 TWIN SABRE BOMBER MOCK UP
DH 100 SPIDER CRAB BECAME VAMPIRE
DH 101 BOMBER (SPEC. B 11/41)
DH 102 SPECIAL NIGHT BOMBER TO SPEC. B 4/42
DH 103 HORNET (SCHEME 3.
AIRSPEED HORSA TROOP GLIDER
MODEL OF FLYING WING JET - LED TO
DH 108 SWALLOW HIGH SPEED AIRCRAFT
MODELS OF UNSPECIFIED JET ENGINES
WERE ALSO MADE.

NELL GWYNNE'S COTTAGE
ENGINE HOUSE AND FUEL STORE
SALISBURY HALL HOUSE
de Havilland's Wartime
Design HQ and home
of the Mosquito.
Airspeed also built
the Horsa Glider
here.

PLOUGHED UP FIELD

LONDON

CHURCHILL'S 'TREE HOUSE'

D.O. & AIRSPEED AIR RAID SHELTERS

W
X
Y   Z
B

ORIGINAL HANGAR
COTTAGES
SECOND HANGAR
WIND PUMP AND A.R.P LOOK-OUT
WORKS AIR RAID SHELTERS
DRAWING OFFICES HUTS 1 & 2
ROUTE OF THE 'BIG PUSH'
TIN BASHERS 'HUT'
AIRSPEED'S' HANGAR
2 ND PROTOTYPE W4052 POSITION PRIOR TO TAKE OFF
FARMER DIXON'S TRACTOR SHORTLY BEFORE T/O

Sketch prepared by de Havilland engineer Alan Copas (who witnessed the events) listing the aircraft developed and built at Salisbury Hall, away from the parent factory at Hatfield that was a potential target for enemy bombers. Three of the five Mosquitoes built at the Hall were flown out of the adjacent field. The take-off of the second prototype, from point Z, was made no easier when farmer Dixon continued ploughing the field, significantly reducing the available take-off run.

Prime Minister Winston Churchill touring the de Havilland factory at Hatfield. In the background is Mosquito constructor's No. 98501, awaiting its Merlin engines.

An impressive example of low flying by a photographic reconnaissance Mosquito P.R. Mk 34. Tests in early 1941 confirmed the Mosquito as the world's fastest operational aircraft, a distinction which it enjoyed for the next two and a half years.

Ground engineers, using minimal specialised equipment, service the port Merlin engine of a Mosquito between flights. The bombers, with speeds of up to 415 mph, could elude most enemy fighters without the need for guns.

Mosquito production at de Havilland's No. 2 factory at Leavesden, near Watford, in 1943. Aircraft HK290 (left foreground) was an N.F. Mk XVII night fighter.

Mosquito fighter bomber. The photograph is signed by Group Captain John Cunningham. As a wartime RAF pilot he led development of the technique of interception by radar, the success of which broke the effectiveness of the German night bombing campaign against Britain. After the war, John Cunningham became chief test pilot at Hatfield, a post he held until his retirement in 1980.

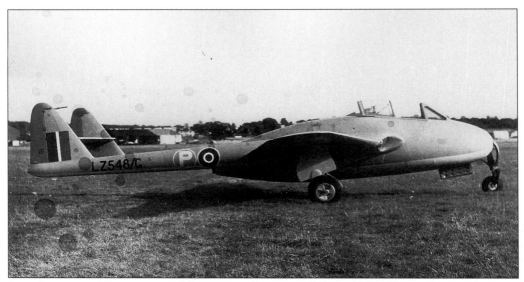

Into the jet age. The prototype Vampire single-seat jet fighter, LZ548/G, on the aerodrome at Hatfield from which the first flight was made by Geoffrey de Havilland Jr on 20 September 1943. Known as the Spidercrab during its highly-secret development, the D.H.100 was the first combat aircraft in the world to attain a speed of more than 500 mph.

The Vampire entered service too late to see any action in the Second World War. This was one of the later F. Mk I fighters, with a pressurised cockpit and one-piece canopy. The Vampire's fuselage remained of wooden construction.

A side-by-side, two-seat training version of the Vampire, known as the D.H.115, was developed in the former Airspeed factory at Christchurch, Hampshire. The RAF chose it as the first jet aircraft on which pilots would qualify for their 'wings' and this T. Mk 11 was still able to display impressive manoeuvrability during Exeter Air Day in June 1963, twenty years after LZ548/G's first flight.

A swarm of no fewer than sixty-seven Tiger Moths is visible in this wartime photograph of the Royal Australian Air Force Training base at Temora. This base was one of five set up in New South Wales under the Empire Air Training Scheme. All had Tiger Moths.

A radar-equipped Mosquito night fighter. Using interception techniques developed by John Cunningham and his navigator, Jimmy Rawnsley, this type was the main deterrent against German air attacks of 1943 which often used bomb-carrying, single-seat fighters in an effort to match the invulnerability of Mosquito bombers. The night-fighter Mosquitoes still caught them!

Experimental annular dive brake fitted to a Mosquito for trials. It was not fitted to operational aircraft.

Four rockets, or 'unrotating projectiles' as they were originally known, under the port wing of a Mosquito. The impact of eight 60 lb rockets was said to be equivalent to a salvo from the 6 inch guns of a Royal Navy cruiser.

Amiens prison in France after a low-level pinpoint attack by Mosquitoes in February 1944 aimed at damaging the barracks and breaching the walls to allow the escape of French Resistance fighters held under sentence of death. Over 250 partisans escaped. Mosquitoes perfected the art of attacking small, specific targets with an accuracy seldom equalled until the advent of 'smart' laser-guided bombs in the 1990s.

The mission symbols painted on the nose of this Mosquito bomber typified the extraordinary performance of this versatile aircraft. Operational losses were in the region of one per cent and several 'Mossies' made more than 150 combat sorties.

By 1943 Mosquito bombers could carry a 4,000 lb bomb all the way to Berlin.

The scene a few minutes before the prototype D.H.103 Hornet, RR915, flew for the first time from Hatfield, on 28 July 1944. The war ended before this scaled-down single-seat development of the Mosquito could enter service.

An unusual wartime task for Mosquitoes was to ferry VIPs and vital components to, and from, Sweden. Bearing civilian markings and flown by airline captains, they could carry half a ton of urgent freight or one passenger inside a special capsule housed in the bomb bay.

Six
Return to Peace

Within six weeks of the surrender of Japan, de Havilland flew its first postwar aeroplane. This was the D.H.104 Dove, a low-wing, twin-engined mini-airliner designed to replace the Rapide. Although faster and able to fly on one engine, the Dove's relatively high purchase price and greater operating costs put it beyond the reach of many small airlines. Even so, Dove sales exceeded 500 to operators around the world.

To obtain operational experience of swept wings, the company built three D.H.108 tailless research aircraft. The first was flown on 15 May 1946, followed by the second on 1 August. Speeds above 600 mph were soon achieved. While making an attempt on the world speed record, the No. 2 D.H.108 broke up in the air, killing its test pilot, Geoffrey de Havilland Jr.

Data from the D.H.108 were used during the design of the company's most ambitious postwar project, the D.H.106 Comet jet airliner, although this had a more traditional configuration. The first public demonstration at Farnborough, in September 1949, was followed by fast overseas flights during which many records were broken or established. The world's first jet airliner flight with fare-paying passengers was made from London to Johannesburg, South Africa, on 2 May 1952, cutting the normal flight time by half.

The airfield at Hatfield was closed in 1994 as part of a rationalisation plan by new owners. Sadly, bad weather prevented the event being marked by a planned fly-in of more than 100 de Havilland light aircraft for 'The Last Great Picnic'.

Sir Geoffrey de Havilland's great Enterprise, established sixty years earlier, was no more, but aircraft of the Age of Adventure continue to delight both their pilots and spectators, and will continue to provoke nostalgic and heroic memories for many years to come.

Previous pages: Tiger Moth coming in to land at Croydon Airport in 1958. On the apron, in front of the control tower and terminal building, are D.H.114 Heron (left) and D.H.104 Dove transports, successors to the Rapide biplane.

Something old, something new. A de Havilland Rapide and three D.H.104 Doves await delivery on the aerodrome at Hatfield. Buildings in the background are still covered in wartime camouflage. The prototype Dove made its first flight only six weeks after the end of the war.

Vampire single-seat jet fighters being built at Chester for export during the early post-war years.

Chief test pilot John Cunningham and the experimental Ghost-engined Vampire TG278 in which he reached 59,492 ft on 23 March 1948, establishing a world record that stood for five years.

D.H.89 Rapide *Lord Roberts*, one of the large fleet of Rapides operated by British European Airways as its 'Islander' class on Scottish, Scilly and Channel Islands routes in the 1950s. Here a nurse disembarks from G-AGUR which has landed on the beach at Barra in the Western Isles, Scotland, on an air ambulance mission.

Authors Maurice Allward (left) and John Taylor, with their wives Alice and Doris, and children Bruce and Susan, at Portsmouth, after chartering a Rapide of Newman Airways in May 1950 to fly from Ryde on the Isle of Wight. The thirteen minute flight cost a total of £4 and was made in worsening weather conditions that grounded other aircraft in the region.

Third prototype of the D.H.108 research aircraft, built in 1946-47 to study the behaviour of swept wings and to provide basic aerodynamic data for the Comet airliner.

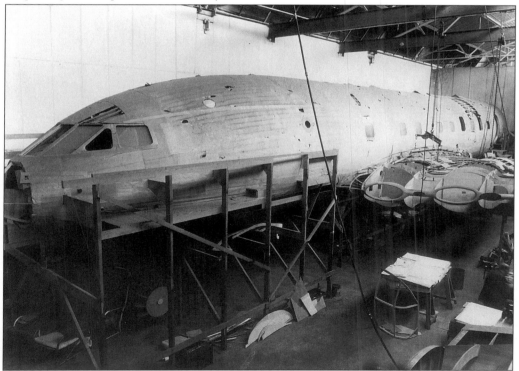

Wooden mockups of the D.H.106 Comet, the world first operational jet airliner, at Hatfield. The four de Havilland Ghost engines fitted to the Comet 1 were built into the wingroots as shown.

The prototype Comet, G-ALVG, taking off for an early test from Hatfield. The single large main undercarriage wheels and rectangular windows of the early version can be seen.

The world's first jet airliner service with fare-paying passengers was made by the thirty-six seat Comet G-ALYP on 2 May 1952, when it flew from London to Johannesburg. The pioneer de Havilland airliner reduced the journey time by half, reaching Johannesburg in 23 hours and 34 minutes.

Hornet Moth flying over club aircraft at Panshanger airfield near Welwyn Garden City. This was the site to which the London Aeroplane Club moved when it was reformed in the late 1940s.

To commemorate the fiftieth anniversary of the MacRobertson Air Race from England to Australia in 1934, this Puss Moth, G-AAZP, built in 1930, was flown by pilots Tim Williams and Henry Labouchere to Melbourne in 1984, along a route following closely that of the race. The time of arrival over the Flemmington race course, planned in 1982, was achieved precisely on time – 3 pm on Saturday 8 December.

Although not an 'official' de Havilland aeroplane, the Puffin manpowered aircraft epitomised the innovative talents of the company's personnel. It was built in 1961 by a group of aerodynamicists and designers, in an attempt to win the £5,000 prize offered by Henry Kremer for the first manpowered aircraft to fly around a figure-of-eight course between two markers half a mile apart. The Puffin did not win the prize but established a record by being pedalled for 993 yards, a distance not exceeded for several years.

Known initially as the Jet Dragon, the D.H.125 was the jet-engined successor to the Dove executive transport. Its relatively roomy six-to-eight-seat cabin and good performance made it a popular choice for customers all over the world. Sales of successively improved versions have exceeded 800 over a quarter of a century.

Author Maurice Allward after his first solo flight on 16 October 1955 in Tiger Moth G-AOBO from Croydon Airport. The less said about the unofficial 'flying suit' – his Royal Observer Corps uniform – the better.

Breakfast patrol, the object of which was to fly and land at a select aerodrome without being 'intercepted'. In loose formation, Tiger Moths fly serenely over the tapestry of the countryside to the target aerodrome. Pilot on this flight was Maurice Allward under the guidance of the legendary instructor Nepean Bishop.

A three-engined D.H.121 Trident airliner of British European Airways being prepared for a night take-off at Heathrow Airport, London.

A D.H.121 Trident makes a demonstration automatic landing with the hands of both pilots away from the controls. The landing system was developed to enable the airliner to operate in conditions which, during three months from November 1958 to January 1959, had caused BEA to cancel 1,370 scheduled services.

The D.H.110 Sea Vixen naval fighter was the final development of the Vampire twin-boom configuration. The first Sea Vixen squadron, No. 892, embarked on HMS *Ark Royal* in February 1960. Armed with infra-red air-to-air missiles, or Bullpup air-to-surface rockets, it was a formidable aircraft, with a performance comparable to that of contemporary land-based fighters.

Some of the participants at a Moth Fly-in at Hatfield in the 1960s.

HM Queen Elizabeth II and HRH Prince Philip disembark from a BAe 146 of The Queen's Flight. Although the Hatfield site was operating under a new name when the aircraft was built, it was produced largely by people who had served with the de Havilland Company, and is generally regarded as the last type to have come from the famous Enterprise.

End of the Enterprise. The Revd Captain Donald Wallace, Chaplain to the de Havilland Moth Club, conducts a Service of Remembrance and Thanksgiving at Hatfield on Easter Monday, 4 April 1994, shortly before the airfield was closed. Bad weather kept away most of the hundred-plus de Havilland aircraft that had been expected at what was called 'The Last Great Picnic'. In the background can be seen the D.H.88 Comet racer of 1934 that was soon to leave Hatfield for its new home with the Shuttleworth Collection of historic aircraft at Old Warden Aerodrome.